Future Tech

The Future of Transportation

Jun Kuromiya

Lerner Publications ◆ Minneapolis

Lerner Publications Company
An imprint of Lerner Publishing Group, Inc.
241 First Avenue North
Minneapolis, MN 55401 USA

For reading levels and more information, look up this title at www.lernerbooks.com.

Main body text set in Adrianna Regular.
Typeface provided by Chank.

Editor: Rebecca Higgins **Photo Editor**: Rebecca Higgins
Designer: Amy Salveson

Library of Congress Cataloging-in-Publication Data

Names: Kuromiya, Jun, 1992– author.
Title: The future of transportation / Jun Kuromiya.
Description: Minneapolis : Lerner Publications, [2021] | Series: Searchlight books.
    Future tech | Includes bibliographical references and index. | Audience: Ages 8–11 |
    Audience: Grades K–1 | Summary: "The fossil fuels powering cars, trains, and planes
    are harming the environment, but scientists are creating innovative, transportation
    solutions. Explore the future of transportation from self-flying drones to levitating
    trains"— Provided by publisher.
Identifiers: LCCN 2019047570 (print) | LCCN 2019047571 (ebook) |
    ISBN 9781541597310 (library binding) | ISBN 9781728400846 (ebook)
Subjects: LCSH: Transportation—Forecasting—Juvenile literature. | Transportation—
    Technological innovations—Juvenile literature. | CYAC: Transportation—Forecasting. |
    Transportation—Technological innovations. | LCGFT: Literature.
Classification: LCC HE152 .M57 2021 (print) | LCC HE152 (ebook) | DDC 388.01/12—
    dc23

LC record available at https://lccn.loc.gov/2019047570
LC ebook record available at https://lccn.loc.gov/2019047571

Manufactured in the United States of America
1-47835-48275-1/14/2020

Contents

Chapter 1

POWER SOURCES

Transportation has a huge effect on our lives. Modern transportation allows people to travel at speeds that would have been unimaginable a century ago. It's easy to forget how quickly things have changed, and soon, travel will be transformed again. Even taking a ride to school won't be the same.

Americans spent 70 billion hours driving in 2017.

Coal-powered trains released harmful chemicals into the air.

Transportation's power sources will change. Humans made the first steam engine using coal as fuel in the eighteenth century. Since then, changes in transportation tend to come at the expense of Earth's ecosystems. Most transportation relies on fossil fuels such as coal and oil. Fossil fuels emit pollutants that contaminate Earth's air. So our methods of transportation contribute to climate change.

Driving Green

Car engineers are inventing green ways to power cars. One solution already on the market is electric cars. These cars don't run on the fossil fuel, gasoline. Instead, they use a rechargeable battery to power the motor.

MOST ELECTRIC CARS CAN GO 100 MILES (161 KM) ON A CHARGE.

Natural gas power plants produce electricity.

But engineers still have a major issue. To produce electricity for batteries, we often rely on natural gas. This is because gas easily produces electricity. As long as we use gas to produce our electricity, using electric cars will burn some fossil fuels. However, the electric cars use nearly three times less fuel than traditional vehicles.

The Stella Era solar car's roof has dark solar panels.

Another option is the solar car. Solar panels on its surface soak up energy from the sun to power its battery. That's perfect for sunny California. But what happens in areas with less sun? Most solar cars use an electric battery to store energy for when it's dark.

Even more promising is the hydrogen car. Toyota, Honda, and other car companies are developing cars that use hydrogen to create electricity. The cars' only emission is water. To get electricity from hydrogen, you need certain metals to trigger a reaction. The first versions of the hydrogen cars used platinum, an expensive metal. But a team in California found a new material that uses cheaper metals, such as cobalt, to make electricity.

Hydrogen is pumped into a hydrogen car's tanks.

Initially, hydrogen cars would be more expensive per gallon than gas vehicles. The added cost would help cover equipment needed for hydrogen cars.

Scientists are still working to overcome many hurdles. One of the biggest concerns is cost. An estimate suggests that building battery charging stations and other equipment for hydrogen vehicles might cost $6 trillion! But hydrogen-fueled engines and other clean technologies provide hope that cars may run much cleaner in the future.

Chapter 2

LOOK, NO HANDS!

Soon cars might drive themselves. Self-driving cars could take the pressure of driving off people. People could get in a car and tell it where they want to go. Self-driving cars could also eliminate car accidents caused by human error.

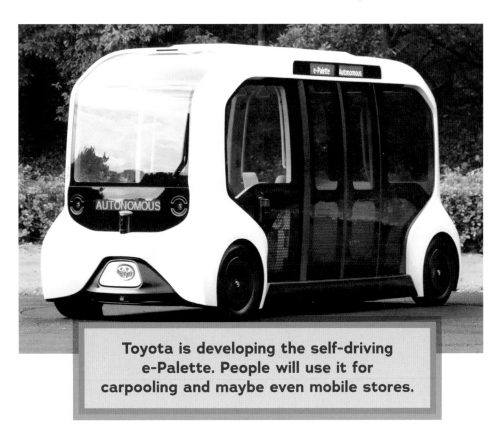

Toyota is developing the self-driving e-Palette. People will use it for carpooling and maybe even mobile stores.

Sensors on the Road

Computer software for self-driving cars doesn't get distracted as human drivers do. But any mistakes in the software's code could have fatal consequences. One study looked at car accidents in California between 2014 and 2018. Eighty-eight accidents involved self-driving cars. However, the study found that in eighty-one of those accidents, the human driver took control of the car and was responsible for the crash.

Cell phone use while driving causes 1.6 million car accidents each year.

Most self-driving cars have options for a human driver to take over operation of the vehicle at any time.

Self-driving cars have cutting-edge technology. They use lasers, radars, and other technology to read their environment. Together, the sensors build a digital 3D map. The car uses the map to navigate roads on its own. It has an internal computer that reads the map and signals how the car should move. The computer uses special algorithms to follow traffic rules. It even accounts for weather and traffic patterns!

Self-driving cars could grant new freedom for people who are elderly or disabled. Many people can't drive on their own. With self-driving cars, they could gain more independence.

The Concept-I RIDE was designed for people who use wheelchairs. It is controlled through joysticks instead of a steering wheel and pedals.

The Future of Ew!

Everyone knows what it's like to be stuck in a car and have to use the bathroom. Some companies are finding solutions. Imagine if your car's seat could double as a toilet. The waste would be stored in the car and disposed later. Long drives and road trips would be more comfortable. Just don't think too much about the smell!

Toilets in your car's seats could reduce the number of stops on a long road trip.

Chapter 3

MAGNETIC LEVITATION

The future of transportation will be faster, especially for trains. Trains don't have to deal with traffic. In theory, there's no limit to their speed. But due to aging technology and high amounts of friction on the tracks, Amtrak trains in the US reach speeds of around 100 to 150 miles (161 to 241 km) an hour. Japan Railway (JR) is working on a train capable of speeds up to about 375 miles (604 km) an hour. How is that possible? The answer is levitation.

Amtrak served 32.5 million passengers in 2019.

Off the Rails

Imagine taking two magnets and pushing their north or south poles together. The two magnets will repel each other. Maglev trains use this technology. Powerful magnets rest on the bottom of the train and the top of the tracks. With the right alignment, the magnets push the train up into the air. In fact, maglev trains float about 5 inches (13 cm) above the tracks.

While north and south poles attract each other, like poles repel the other. Maglev trains use like poles to move forward.

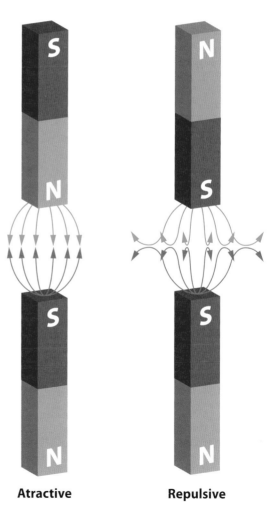

Atractive   **Repulsive**

These same magnets move the train along the tracks. Using electricity, the track alternates the magnetic poles of the magnets. While one magnet pushes the train, the other magnet pulls the train. This push and pull cause the train to move forward. With no wheels and less friction than traditional trains, maglev trains can move at incredible speeds.

JR is already trying to bring maglev trains to the US. Imagine a 40-mile (64 km) train ride from Washington, DC, to Baltimore, Maryland, taking just fifteen minutes!

JR'S MAGLEV TRAIN IS ALMOST THREE TIMES FASTER THAN AN AMTRAK TRAIN.

Unfortunately, maglev trains and their tracks are very expensive to make. The 40-mile (64 km) track from Washington, DC, to Baltimore would cost $15 billion. Some people are protesting this cost. They worry that tickets on such an expensive train would cost too much for many travelers.

In 2007, people in Germany protested installation of a maglev train because of its cost.

STEM Spotlight

Researchers have pushed maglev technology further with the hyperloop. It uses magnets to propel travelers in pods through a vacuum tube. Vacuums have very low air resistance. That means the pods can move incredibly fast. How fast? Virgin Hyperloop One's prototype reaches 670 miles (1,078 km) an hour. That is faster than the average commercial airplane! A team in China successfully used a vacuum tube to run a maglev train at 1,800 miles (2,897 km) an hour.

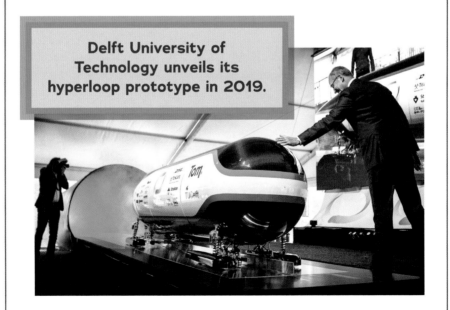

Delft University of Technology unveils its hyperloop prototype in 2019.

Chapter 4

UP IN THE AIR

Though airplanes were invented one hundred years ago, they are still one of the fastest modes of travel. While most planes are unlikely to get faster in the future, flying will become much more common.

There were one billion airline passengers in 2018.

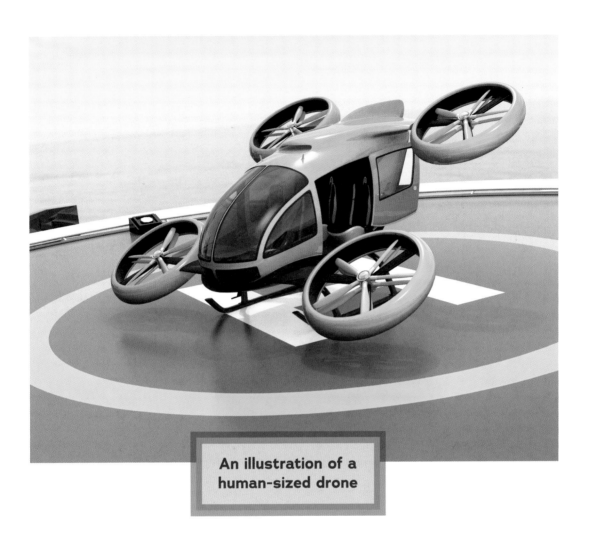

An illustration of a
human-sized drone

Drones in the Sky

Flight might become a daily activity for the average
person, thanks to self-flying drones. Some companies
are creating human-sized drones. These drones could
make it possible to transport humans in the air without
a pilot.

A full-sized prototype of Volocopter displayed in Singapore.

In Dubai, a company is experimenting with Volocopter, a flying taxi service. The service would be similar to ride-share apps such as Uber or Lyft, except it would avoid traffic on the streets. Eventually, the drones would use sensory technology such as self-driving cars to avoid obstacles in the air.

Drones would be fast too. For example, EHang's flying taxi could fly up to 80 miles (129 km) an hour. That's definitely faster than city traffic, which is often limited to 20 miles (32 km) an hour. As with many new inventions, the service would initially be quite expensive. But if it becomes cheaper, it could help clear traffic jams. With travel time cut down, travelers could have more time to hang out with friends and family.

EHANG FLIES DURING A PREVIEW IN 2019.

As the technology improves, more companies will deliver goods by drones. Shipping will be faster and cheaper. People won't have to worry about going to the store.

Drones carrying packages may become more common in the future.

Drones could provide aid to people right after a hurricane.

Faster travel could also have a significant effect on people suffering from natural disasters. Storms often wash out roads and restrict travel. But drones carrying food or medical supplies could easily go to remote locations at a much lower cost than traditional vehicles. Drones could be lifesaving for victims of natural disasters.

Scientists are trying to find a transportation plan that solves a variety of challenges.

The future of transportation is exciting. Scientists are working on new technologies that will change the ways you move around the world. No matter who you are or where you come from, future transportation will transform your life.

STEM Spotlight

In 2018, US airlines alone burned almost 18 billion gallons (68 billion L) of fuel. To combat this, various companies are trying to create passenger airplanes powered by electricity. Current prototypes can't travel as far as commercial airplanes or carry as many people. But researchers predict that within the next twenty years, commercial electric airplanes will become available. Imagine flying across the ocean on battery energy!

Boeing created this passenger plane to test electric flight.

Glossary

algorithm: a set of steps and rules designed for a computer to follow

drone: a flying vehicle without a pilot

ecosystem: a network of living things and their environment

fossil fuel: a natural resource of energy formed over millions of years by the breakdown of living things

platinum: a valuable silver-colored metal

pollutant: a substance that contaminates

prototype: an early sample or copy of a tool or machine

software: programs and algorithms used by a computer to perform functions

steam engine: an engine powered by steam

vacuum: an empty space without any air or gas

Learn More about the Future of Transportation

Books

Hirsch, Rebecca E. *Climate Change and Energy Technology.* Minneapolis: Lerner Publications, 2019. Learn about how new energy technology is combating climate change.

Jefferis, David. *Space Tourists: Vacations across the Universe.* New York: Crabtree, 2018. Travel to space and explore other planets.

Wood, John. *Travel Technology: Maglev Trains, Hovercrafts, and More.* New York: Gareth Stevens, 2018. Deep dive into the world of maglev trains, hovercrafts, and much more.

Websites

Energy Kids
https://www.eia.gov/kids
Discover what energy is, how it works, and how it impacts you.

Kiddle: Alternative Fuel Vehicle Facts
https://kids.kiddle.co/Alternative_fuel_vehicle
Learn about alternatives to fossil fuels and how they are powering vehicles

Kinooze: Maglev Train
http://kinooze.com/a-train-as-fast-as-an-aeroplane-maglev-train/
Explore the science behind these levitating trains.

Index

Photo Acknowledgments

Image credits: DANNY HU/Getty Images, p. 4; Alan Tunnicliffe Photography/Getty Images, p. 5; joel-t/Getty Images, p. 6; Ron and Patty Thomas/Getty Images, p. 7; Mark Evans/Getty Images, p. 8; Tramino/Getty Images, pp. 9-10; Kyodo News/Getty Images, p. 11; Tero Vesalainen/Getty Images, p. 12; metamorworks/Getty Images, p. 13; Robert Hradil/Getty Images, p. 14; joshuaraineyphotography/Getty Images, p. 15; StonePhotos/Getty Images, p. 16; NoPainNoGain/Shutterstock.com, p. 17; Xinhua News Agency/Getty Images, pp. 18, 24; the.epic.man/Getty Images, p. 19; Johannes Simon/Getty Images, p. 20; ROBIN VAN LONKHUIJSEN/Getty Images, p. 21; Aaron Foster/Getty Images, p. 22; Chesky_W/Getty Images, p. 23; JOE KLAMAR/Getty Images, p. 25; Maxiphoto/Getty Images, p. 26; Science Photo Library-NASA/Getty Images, p. 27; Stígur Már Karlsson/Heimsmyndir/Getty Images, p. 28; NurPhoto/Getty Images, p. 29.

Cover: Pavel Chagochkin/Shutterstock.com.